GRACE PALEY

Begin Again

GRACE PALEY is a writer and a teacher, a feminist and an activist. Her most recent book, *Just As I Thought*, is a collection of her personal and political essays and articles. In 1994, her *Collected Stories* was a finalist for the National Book Award. She lives in New York City and Vermont.

Begin Again

GRACE PALEY

BEGIN AGAIN

Collected

Poems

Farrar Straus Giroux

New York

Farrar, Straus and Giroux
18 West 18th Street, New York 10011

Printed in the United States of America
Published in 2000 by Farrar, Straus and Giroux
First paperback edition, 2001

Some of the poems in this collection were first published, some in slightly different
versions, in the following books: Leaning Forward (Granite Press, 1985), 365
Reasons Not to Have Another War (War Resisters League, 1989), Long Walks
and Intimate Talks (The Feminist Press, 1991), New and Collected Poems
(Tilbury House, 1992) and magazines: Chelsea, Field, Ikon, Persea,
Shankpainter, Sunbury, Win Magazine, Alaska Quarterly Review,
Women and Art.
"What would happen" was issued as a broadside in a letterpress limited edition
under the title "Goldenrod" (Granite Press, 1983).
"Families" and "On the Ramblas A Tree A Girl" are reprinted by permission of
The Feminist Press at the City University of New York from Long Walks and
Intimate Talks by Grace Paley, 1991.

The Library of Congress has cataloged the hardcover edition as follows:
Paley, Grace.
Begin again: collected poems / Grace Paley.— 1st ed.
p. cm.
ISBN-13: 978-0-374-12642-1 (alk. paper)
ISBN-10: 0-374-12642-9 (alk. paper)
I. Title.

PS3566.A46 A17 2000
811'.54—dc21

99046996

Paperback ISBN-13: 978-0-374-52724-2
Paperback ISBN-10: 0-374-52724-5

www.fsgbooks.com

P1

The publisher and author would like to extend special thanks to Bea Gates for extracting many of
the poems in this book from Grace Paley's notebooks.
And special thanks to Jane Cooper.

For Bob

For Jeanne, my sister

Contents

I

III / THETFORD POEMS

I V

V

VI / BEGIN AGAIN

I

A woman invented fire and called it
                    the wheel
Was it because the sun is round
          I saw the round sun bleeding to sky
And fire rolls across the field
          from forest to treetop
It leaps like a bike with a wild boy riding it

oh   she said
          see the orange wheel of heat
light that took me from the
          window of my mother's home
to home in the evening

Stanzas: *Old Age and the Conventions of Retirement Have Driven My Friends from the Work They Love*

1

When she was young she wanted
to sing in a bank
a song about money
   the lyrics of gold
was her song
   she dressed for it

2

She did good. She stood up like a
planted flower among yellow weeds
   turning to please the sun
   they were all shiny
it was known she was planted

3

No metaphor reinvents the job of the nurture of children
except to muddy or mock.

4

The job of hunting of shooting in hunting season of
standing alone in the woods of being an Indian

5

The municipal center
the morning of anger
the centrifugal dream
her voice flung out on plates of rage
          then they were put in a paper sack
          she was sent to the china closet
          and never came back

6

Every day he went out, forsaking
wife and child
with his black bag he accompanied
the needle of pain as it
sewed our lives to death

7

One day at work   he cried
I am in my full powers
          suddenly he was blind
when slabs of time and aperture returned
dear friend   we asked
          what do you see
he said   I only see what has been
          seen already

One day when I was a child   long ago
Mr. Long Ago spoke up in school
He said
Oh children you must roll your r's
no no not on your tongue little girl
IN YOUR THROAT
there is nothing so beautiful as r rolled in the throat of a French
    woman
no woman more beautiful
he said   looking back
            back
            at beauty

Drowning (I)

If I were in the middle of the Atlantic
     drowning   far from home
I would look up at the sky
     veil of my hiding life
and say:
     goodbye

then I would sink

the second time I'd come up   I'd say
     these are the willful waves of the watery sea
     which is drowning me
then I would sink
the third time I'd come up   it would be my last
     my arms   reaching
     my knees   falling
I'd cry   oh   oh
     first friend of my thinking head
     dear flesh
     farewell

Drowning (II)

This is how come I am drowned:
 First the sun shone on me
 Then the wind blew over me
 Then the sand polished me
 Then the sea touched me
 Then the tide came

Life

Some people set themselves tasks
other people say   do anything   only live
still others say
        oh oh   I will never forget you   event of my first life

Right Now

The women let the tide go out
                    which will return   which will return
the sand   the salt   the fat drowned babies
The men ran furiously
                    along the banks of the estuary
screaming
                    Come back you fucking sea
right now
                    right now

A Poem about Storytelling

The artist comes next
she tells the story of the stories

The first person may be the child who
says   Listen!   Guess what happened!
The important listener is the mother
The mother says   What?

The first person can be the neighbor
She says   Today my son told me   Goodbye
I said   Really?   Who are you?   You
didn't even say hello yet   The listener
is probably her friend   She remembers
Well wasn't he always like that   as a small boy
I mean   The neighbor says   That's not
true   You're absolutely wrong   He was like a
motorcycle   a little horse   every now
and then at rest   a flower

The first person is often the lover who
says   I never knew anyone like you
The listener is the beloved   She whispers
Who?   Me?

The first person is the giver of testimony
He rises and tells   I lived in that village
My father shouted   He returned from the fields
I was too small   My father cried out
Why don't you grow up and help me   My mother said
Help him   you're eight years old   it's time
The listeners say   Oh! it was just
like that   I remember

The giver of testimony rises and tells
I lived in the hut   behind the barn
The padrone   the manager   the master came
to me   I can take you whenever I want
he said   Now you're old enough   The right
age is twelve he said   The giver of testimony
rises   She looks into her village   She
looks into the next village   Where
are the listeners

The artist comes next   She waits for
the listeners too   What if they're all dead or
deafened by grief or in prison   Then
there's no way out of it   She will listen
It's her work   She will be the listener
in the story of the stories

A Warning

One day I forgot Jerusalem and my right arm is withered
My right arm, my moving arm, my rising and falling arm
                    my loving arm
Is withered

And my left eye, the blinker and winker is plucked out
It hangs by six threads of endless remembering.
Because I forgot Jerusalem
And wherever I go, I am known, I am recognized at once. I am
                    perceived by strangers.
Because on one day, only one day I forgot Jerusalem.

Jews everywhere, Jews, old deaths of the north and south
                    kingdoms,
Poor Jews in the ghetto walls built by the noble Slav,
                    Jew princes
In Amsterdam who live in diamond houses that shine like window-
                    panes
Listen to me. Wherever you go, keep the nation of that city
                    in mind
For I forgot her and now I am blind and crippled.

Even my lover   a Christian with pale eyes and the barbarian's
        foreskin
                    has left me.

Alive

The veins that stand on the back of my sunburned hand
are something like the branched veins on the flat tan
                              shore of the bay
Out of these, when the tide tugs
salt sea runs   back
into the rocky basin from which
we came
on the first day   specks
in a stranded pool dashed
in high tide   alive
on the hot dry land.

At the Battery

I am standing on one foot
at the prow of great Manhattan
leaning forward
projecting a little into the bright harbor

If only a topographer in a helicopter
would pass over my shadow
I might be imposed forever
on the maps of this city

An Arboreal Mystery

On Jane Street in October
I saw three ginkgo trees
    the first is naked to the bony branch
    the second is a dance of little golden fans
    the third is green as green September

20th Street   Spring

the wives of the black-sailed seminarians
take their children to walk with green pails

they are light-haired and slim   their husbands are studying
passion and service   the seminary

is old   the baby leaves of the old sycamores are pale green
are river yellow   like the high light arms of the sycamore

the seminary is red and soot-darkened
by the soot-making city   it is at the side of the city near the river

it stands aside from the piers and the warehouses and the
        longshoremen
it intends to be quiet and dark   though sunlight surrounds it

sun lies on the streets and the lawns and the children
of the seminarians play with red hoops in the street in the sun

note to grandparents

the children are healthy
    the children are rosy
we take them to the park
    we take them to the playground

they swing on the swings
    the wind smacks their faces
they jump and are lively
    they eat everything

they sleep without crying
    they are very smart
each day they grow
    you would hardly know them

psalm

their shoes are stuccoed with sawdust and blood
the two young butchers walk singing together on Ninth Avenue
the sun is out because it is the lunch hour
they kick the melting snow and splash into deep puddles
then they embrace one another in the cold air
for water and singing may wash away the blood of the lamb

Mulberry Street

Mulberry Street ends in good works
The Committee for Nonviolent Action begins there
Also St. Barnabas House which shelters abandoned children

And on the corner of Mott Street
Bob Nichols is making a playground
single-handed   two mountains   an iron tower from which
the cliffs of Houston Street can be observed
a maple glade   a ship at sea

War

The boys from St. Bernard's
and the boys from
Our Lady of Pompeii
converge on the corner of Bleecker and Bank

There is a grinding of snowballs
and a creaking of ice

The name of our Lord is invoked

But for such healthy tough warriors
He has other deaths in mind

Sulky
They part

For Danny

My son enters the classroom
There are thirty-two children waiting for him
He dreams that he will teach them to read
His head is full of the letters that words are looking for

Because of his nature
his fingers are flowers
Here is a rose   he says   look   it grew right
into the letter R

They like that idea very much   they lean forward
He says   now spell garden
They write it correctly in their notebooks   maybe
          because the word rose is in it

My son is happy
Now spell sky
For this simple word the children
turn their eyes down and away   doesn't he know
the city has been quarreling with the sky all of their lives

Well, he says   Spell home   he's a little frightened
          to ask this of them   What?
They laugh   they can't hear him say
What's so funny?   they jump
up out of their seats laughing

My son says hopefully   It's three o'clock
but they don't want to leave   where will they go?
they want to stay right here in the classroom   they probably
want to spell garden again   they want
to examine his hand

The Nature of This City

Children walking with their grandmothers
talk foreign languages
that is the nature of this city
and also this country

Talk is cheap but comes in variety
and witnessing dialect
there is a rule for all
and in each sentence a perfect grammar

On the Fourth Floor

The woman on the fourth floor said   You slut!   don't you knock on my
            door   stand up straight   be a woman!
The girl said   I ain't a slut   I didn't have no father   my mother . . .
The woman said   Stop that   neither did I   I didn't have nothin
The girl said   I ain't a slut   I don't fuck guys
The woman said   Who cares about guys   you're disgusting   you ain't
            a woman
You're dirty   look at you   you can't keep your eyes open

The boy came to the head of the stairs   He hollered   Diana come up
            here   where's the Tuinals
The girl said   I ain't got them
The boy screamed   I had sixteen   I ate ten   I give you four   there's
            two left someplace
I ain't got them   I only got two methadone
Look at you   the boy said   you hung down to the ground   you ate
            them
I didn't   she said   come with me Eddie
to the East River Drive   there's a party   I'll say you're my husband
The boy screamed   Get me the two Tuinals

The woman took the girl's hand   Go into your house   right this
            minute   pay him no mind
wash up   you stink   comb your hair   straight yourself
ain't you ashamed?   Be a woman

Winter Afternoon

Old men and women walk by my window
they're frightened   it's icy wintertime
they take small steps   they're looking
at their feet   they're glad to be
going   they hate
the necessity

sometimes the women wear heels   why
do they do this   the old women's
heads are bent   they see their shoes
which are often pointy   these shoes
were made for crossed legs in the
evening   pointing

                sometimes the old men
walk a dog   the dog moves too fast
the man stands still   the dog stands
still   the smells come to the dog
floating from the square earth of the
plane tree   from the tires of cars
at rest   all this interesting life
and adventure comes to the waiting dog
the man doesn't know this   the street
is too icy   old women in pointy shoes
and high heels pass him   their necks
in fur collars bent   their eyes watch
their small slippery feet

Middle-Age Poem

With what joy
I left home to deposit one thousand, one hundred and nineteen
dollars in the bank
I was whistling and skipping
you would think I had a new baby and a new cradle
after so many years
or that my mother had come to visit from Queens, borough of
cemeteries
you would think a lover
was waiting
at the corner of Chemical Trust
and First National
right under the willow oak
with open arms

Bob Visits Friends

Well I can see you now
you are hurrying along the street
head down in order to not miss
any great event on the pavement   you are
about to make a visit to somebody's life
Peter and Elka's   where the children
will welcome you with bread and strawberries
they fly to a proper distance
nibbling rye crumbs by the healthy ton
sighing in Russian and singing in German

Then you will extricate yourself
from the richness of kitchens and family
and cross town again because it's so early
the summer's first light hot hand
has made you feverish for encounter in air
at least by open window   so now the sixth floor
overlooking Bedford Street   the open lot
that will not become the Broome Street Expressway

Because of this political victory and the birth
of a child there is a plan being made
in that small apartment
                    TO BE GOOD AND HAPPY FOREVER
The fact is   this *can* be successful
if it starts late enough in life

On Mother's Day

I went out walking
in the old neighborhood

Look! more trees on the block
forget-me-nots all around them
ivy   lantana shining
and geraniums in the window

Twenty years ago
it was believed that the roots of trees
would insert themselves into gas lines
then fall   poisoned   on houses and children

or tap the city's water pipes   starved
for nitrogen   obstruct the sewers

In those days in the afternoon I floated
by ferry to Hoboken or Staten Island
then pushed the babies in their carriages
along the river wall   observing Manhattan
See Manhattan I cried   New York!
even at sunset it doesn't shine
but stands in fire   charcoal to the waist

But this Sunday afternoon on Mother's Day
I walked west   and came to Hudson Street   tricolored flags
were flying over old oak furniture for sale
brass bedsteads   copper pots and vases
by the pound from India

Suddenly before my eyes   twenty-two transvestites
in joyous parade stuffed pillows
under their lovely gowns

and entered a restaurant
under a sign which said   All Pregnant Mothers Free

I watched them place napkins over their bellies
and accept coffee and zabaglione

I am especially open to sadness and hilarity
since my father died as a child
one week ago in this his ninetieth year

Housing

Walking along a street in a neighborhood
where the black trash bags are stacked as neat
as a woodpile in Vermont   my lover said to me
oh will we ever live in a district like this
where the artists are growing old in brownstones
and their grandchildren visit them with watercolors
and pastels   if we could only find a
condominium or a co-op like the one
on Ninth Street where the tenants themselves
have lovingly laid a mulch of pine branches
among the roses

                then I answered her
it is probably too late for sentiment
of that kind   we are fated to create
our own community in the borough of
Brooklyn   or Staten Island   though there are
many who are happy in the little cities
across the river in another state
where we might well establish patterns of
comfort and gently rising affluence
all of which requires of course that the earth
be not blown up or irremediably
poisoned and that you and I remain if not
lovers at least cordial creators of
family and continuity

Having Arrived by Bike at Battery Park

I thought I would
sit down at one of those park department tables
and write a poem honoring
the occasion which is May 25th
Evelyn   my best friend's birthday
and Willy Langbauer's birthday

Day! I love you for your delicacy
in appearing after so many years
as an afternoon in Battery Park right
on the curved water
where Manhattan was beached

At once arrows
straight as Broadway were driven
into the great Indian heart

Then we came from the east
seasick and safe the
white tormented people
grew fat in the
blood of that wound

II

Whistlers

A stranger calling a dog whistled
and I came running though I am not an afghan

or a high-class poodle and not much like a
city boy's dog with a happy wild tail and red eyes

The stranger said   Excuse me I was calling my dog not you
Ah   I replied to this courteous explanation

Sometimes I whistle too   but mostly for fear
of missing the world   I am a dog to whistlers

For George (I)

What was left   before crumbling
was sweetness in the maple leaf

in our friend George   a brilliant
attentive sweetness

in the wild red maple leaf
before winter   in our friend
George Dennison   before death

For George (II)

The birds everywhere are talking
     about my friend George who is dying
What have the birds to do with it?
In their whistling songs they say   go south
     or else
George   they peck at his window in Maine
     in the town of Temple
Go south   come with us   save yourself
     there's still time
But he refuses to leave   pain has trapped him
Pain keeps him at home

But if he had help?   If the children
whom he has after all immortalized in stories
     of their joyfulness with horses
if the children could help   if Mabel
     would help   if they stopped listening
to George's pain   if they saw the birds
how sure of themselves they are as they wrap up
     their northern affairs
and gather their swarming communities to fly
float   sail   toward long sunlight
     south   south

Certain Days

On certain days I am not in love
and my heart turns over

        crowding the lungs for
        air

        driving blood in and out of
        the skull   improving my mind

        working muscles to the bone

        dashing resonance out of a roaring sea
        at my nerve endings

Not much is needed

        air

        good sense

        power

        a noisy taking in and a
        loud giving back

Then my heart like any properly turned
motor takes off in sparks   dragging all that machinery
through the blazing day
        like grass
                which our lord knows
                I am

One Day

One day   lying on my stomach in the afternoon   trying to sleep
I suffered penis envy (much to
                    my surprise

and with no belief in Freud   for years
                    in fact   extreme
antipathy)   what could I do but turn around

and close my eyes and dream of summer
                    in those days I
                    was a boy   I whistled
at the gate for Tom

Then I woke up
then I slept
and dreamed another dream

in my drowned father's empty pocket
there were nine dollars and the salty sea
he said   I know you   my darling girl
you're the one that's me

The Five-Day Week

The five-day week was set like a firecracker
The five-day week   ah   like a long bath in the
                first bathtub of God
The five-day week was sunny all year   (I remember)
The five-day week gave at last what she'd always longed for
                a cheerful noisy companion
                to Sabbath calm Queen of days

Some Days

Some days I am lonesome   I want to talk to my mother
And she isn't home
Then I ask my father   Where has she been the last twenty years?
And he answers
Where do you think   you fool as usual?
> She is asleep in Abraham's bosom
> Resting from years of your incessant provocation
> Exhausted by infinite love of me
> Escaping from the boredom of days shortening to
> Christmas and the pain of days lengthening to
> Easter
> You know where she is   She is at ease in Zion with all
> the other dead Jews

Vengeance

I cannot keep my mind on Jerusalem
It wanders off like an idiot with no attention span
to whatever city lies outside my window that day
    Damascus
    the libraries of Babylonia
Oh! the five exogamous boroughs of
our beloved home   New York

What will happen
when the Lord
remembers vengeance
(which is his)
and finds me

Family

My father was brilliant   embarrassed   funny   handsome
my mother was plain   serious   principled   kind
my grandmother was intelligent   lonesome for her
                    other life   her dead children   silent
my aunt was beautiful   bitter   angry   loving

I fell among these adjectives in earliest childhood
and was nearly buried with opportunity
some of them stuck to me   others
finding me American and smooth slipped away

Letter

I am writing to the
Chinese Association for the Study
of Jewish Literature

They have asked for the addresses
of a couple of other Jews
Ozick and Kazin to be specific

Of course there are hundreds
probably thousands now alive
writing in Spanish and Portuguese

Russian   even German   the great languages
of nations into whose histories
we were admitted and began almost

immediately to talk   exclaim   praise
make metaphor   despair   raise children
ask questions of the authorities

in their own tongue!   succeed   multiply
and finally be driven out

They say a thousand Jews fled Bombay
in the 12th century   traveled to
Kaifeng City to live in the center

of China   to live   to live   ah   into
the generations they disappeared
in the terrible Yahweh-defying act
of assimilation

My Mother: 33 Years Later

1

There are places
  garden
  music room
  stove
  dining room

Deathbed   her eyes are open   she doesn't speak
  My sister and I hold up a picture of Frannie the first grandchild
  Mama do you know who this is?
  Fools! Who do you think you're talking to?
  Oh!   she cried and turned away

My room   she says
  I've heard that expression
  I know how you talk
  don't think I'm so dumb
  hot pants! that's what you say, you girls!

Bobby and I are walking, arm in arm, across the camp field
Our mothers are behind us. We're nine years old.
We're wearing swimming trunks.
                                    She says
    look   see the line of soft soft
    hair along their spines
    like down   our little birds

One of the mothers
the mother out of whose body
I easily appeared

Once I remembered her

2

This is what I planned:
To get to the end of our life quickly

And begin again

Everyone is intact   talking
Mother and Father   Mira   Babashka
all of us eating our boiled egg
but the poplar tree on Hoe Avenue
has just been cut down and the Norway maple
is planted in Mahopac

Then
my mother gives me
a vase full of zinnias
"as straight as little Russian soldiers"

Yes
mama
as straight as the second grade
in the P.S. 50 schoolyard
at absolute attention
under its woolen hats
of pink   orange   lavender   yellow

On the Bank Street Pier

In the mind's eye
    the mind cries I I I
the mother's face
    the father's looking eye
then sees
    then says
the scrambled iron piers
    the river's broad as
    mother's face

In the mind's ear
    talk   talk   talk
    the tickling tongue
of strangers

Gift

Poets!
Madness is a gift
god-given
(though not to me)

the receiver
knows the secret exit
he need never
plan on death
the door open to all

sometimes
before my very eyes
I see him
slipping the lock
he winks
my gifted friend
he says   don't
take any wooden lovers
while I'm gone

lonesome
I bang on the door
of his locked kingdom

No Love

no love cried the last fling
    in the vase
        on the piano
no love
    her dress like a garden
        her knees
        in the water

her dress
    white peacocks with green tails

is that beautiful she said
            beautiful he said
            touching the marigold's dust

Words

What has happened?
language eludes me
the nice specifying
words of my life fail
when I call

Ah says a friend
dried up no doubt
on the desiccated
twigs in the swamp
of the skull like
a lake where the
water level has been
shifted by highways
a couple of miles off

Another friend says
No no   my dear   perhaps
you are only meant to
speak more plainly

Quarrel

We quarreled
Alone I
turned away
from her dear
face   then I
feared death

Question

Do you think old people should be put away
the one red rheumy eye   the pupil that goes back and back
the hands are scaly
                    do you think all that should be hidden

do you think young people should be seen so much on Saturday
        nights
hunting and singing in packs the way they do
standing on street corners looking this way and that

or the small children who are visible all the time everywhere
and have nothing to do but be smart
but be athletes
but jump
but climb high fences
                    do you think hearts should sink
                    do you think the arteries ought to crumble
                    when they could do good?
because the heart was made to endure
                    why does it not endure?
                    do you think this is the way it should be?

Old Age Porch

All morning they store suns
against the grave
         but this is useless
if you have ever seen a dead person
         you know it

Your friend lies in darkness   all
that sunlight spilled around her
in the watery rays   you make a song
you invent the days
         of friendship

Fund Appeal

Against
    darkness
I send
    money
to the
    American
    Federation
    for the Blind

praying
    not so much
    to be spared
pain
    but for grap-
    pling nerve
    when I come

out of
    all arrival
    to the departure
    of senses.

For My Friend Who Planted
a Tree for His Daughter Jane

Up here we don't plant trees   sometimes we take them down
we want to give back the cleared land   the farmers' hard work long ago

Because the forest moves easily on its red sumac and wild cherry toes
and near the pond the alder and willow stretch toward the tall reeds

They hold the swamp in place for a few years
then they lie down themselves and thicken the earth

So I have looked for a standing tree to call it   Jane

lovely child of my beloved friend   apple tree planted
one year ago   I think you are Jane's tree

apple tree of earliest apples   apple tree of
the summer farmer who sees winter only once in a while

In the cleared field you stand   hemlock and pine
not too far off   and the birch tree   familiar

as the face of our Russian grandparents   white
as their friendly ghosts   I will say   Jane   in August

when the pale apples are ready   then we return
the core to earth   after frost the late apples

redden   grow tart with time and the cold nights   we look west
toward the valley villages   the small orchard   the fruit

early and late tumbled under light snow
sweet mulch of this sweet earth

Responsibility

It is the responsibility of society to let the poet be a poet
It is the responsibility of the poet to be a woman
It is the responsibility of the poet to stand on street corners
        giving out poems and beautifully written leaflets
        also leaflets they can hardly bear to look at
        because of the screaming rhetoric
It is the responsibility of the poet to be lazy   to hang out and
        prophesy
It is the responsibility of the poet not to pay war taxes
It is the responsibility of the poet to go in and out of ivory
        towers and two-room apartments on Avenue C
        and buckwheat fields and army camps
It is the responsibility of the male poet to be a woman
It is the responsibility of the female poet to be a woman
It is the poet's responsibility to speak truth to power as the
        Quakers say
It is the poet's responsibility to learn the truth from the
        powerless
It is the responsibility of the poet to say many times: there is no
        freedom without justice and this means economic
        justice and love justice
It is the responsibility of the poet to sing this in all the original
        and traditional tunes of singing and telling poems
It is the responsibility of the poet to listen to gossip and pass it
        on in the way storytellers decant the story of life
There is no freedom without fear and bravery   there is no
        freedom unless
        earth and air and water continue and children
        also continue
It is the responsibility of the poet to be a woman   to keep an eye on
        this world and cry out like Cassandra, but be
        listened to this time

III

Thetford
Poems

Fear

I am afraid of nature
because of nature   I am mortal

my children and my grandchildren
are also mortal

I lived in the city for forty years
in this way I escaped fear

Families

The sheep families are out in the meadow
Caddy and her two big lambs   Gruff and Veronica
Veronica raises her curly head   then bends to the grass
Usefully she shits green grass and wool is her work

Gruff is going away   he will become something else
Father of generations?   What?   more likely meat   that
is a male in war or pasture   his work is meat

Goldenrod

What would happen
if there were a terrific shortage of goldenrod
in the world
and I put my foot outside this house
to walk in my garden and show city visitors
my two lovely rosebushes
and three remarkable goldenrod plants
that were doing well this year

I would say: Look!
how on each of several sprigs
there are two three dozen tiny stems
and on each stem three four tiny golden
flowers   petals stamen pistil and the pollen
which bees love
                but insufficiently
otherwise
                can you imagine the fields
on rainy days in August   brass
streaking the lodged hay heads
dull brass in the rain
and under the hot sun
the golden flowers
                floating   gold dust of August fields
for miles and miles

ĸ

What is this whiteness on the field?
                    not rime
or the Lord's snowy reason for exploding summer
it is the mist
              that starts the day
with drinks for all

When the wild strawberry leaves turn
red and show the dark place of the strawberries
it is too late

I know this has a
meaning inside my own life
inside dark life

Then

Vera stopped at the flower called fireweed
three fireweed in that old field   year after year
I watch from the kitchen window   I wonder

when the earth is a repository of seed   a seed bank   a
bed where seed rest comfortably   some say for years
waiting for the nudge from weather and light   year after

year   there are three fireweed   no more no less   then
Vera disappeared into the woods and our dog Bear
followed her   I said to myself   WORK! and walked

east toward the far sunny haze of Smarts Mountain   down
into the swale   which had gathered vervain boneset and
meadowsweet   where were the beginnings of those late

asters that should have started their leaves toward
blue and lavender September   still we are the gardeners
of this world and often talk about giving wildness

its chance   it's I who cut the field too late   too
early   right on time   and therefore out of the earth which
is a darkness of timed seed and waiting root the sunlight

chose vervain   jewelweed   boneset   just beyond
our woodchuck-argued garden a great nation of ants
has lived for fifteen years in a high sandy anthill

which I honor with looking and looking and never disrupt
(nor have I learned their lesson of stubborn industry)
they ask nothing except to be not bothered and I personally

agree   though it is my nation that has refined sugar
in bowls of sugar   far from their sandy home   I've often
found them   drunk and bathing

(64)

In Deepest Summer

the milkweed flower
dries to pod   in autumn
flies like seed and dies
in earth and is reborn

but not until
disaster strikes the field
and lays the grasses down
under the weighty ice
in which the water lives

Saint-John's-wort!
it must be summertime
buttercup   gone
hawkweed   gone

black-eyed Susan
        before you
know it   Queen Anne's lace

goldenrod   and that
will be that

A bee!
drowning in
a wild rose
     flat on its
     round back
     kicking
too young to
use love for
health and
enrichment

An ant!
lugging half an ounce
of carcass across
the cement porch steps
he's lost
he struggled back and forth
he carries a feast
for his family
We can't find them
we looked under the steps
there wasn't a stray nation
anywhere

K

False strawberry is
an authentic five-
petaled flower stand-

ing in a whirl of
three strawberry leaves
waiting in disturbed

fields for an accu-
mulation of the
healthy soil that kills

September

Then the flowers became very wild
because it was early September
and they had nothing to lose
they tossed their colors every
which way over the garden wall
splattering the lawn   shoving their
wild orange red rain-disheveled faces
into my window without shame

The Choir Singing

From the balcony of the Thetford Hill
First Congregational Church
I look down at the choir singing
the adoration of Christ their Lord
the high foreheads of the older women
shine   why!   that's the condition of
my own forehead which seemed in the
bathroom mirror to appear unusually
intelligent this morning   the delicate
daily hair loss contributing to the
reality and appearance of wisdom

Leaves   Apples

The golden maples had not yet begun their work
on behalf of beauty   the reds   like flowers
had sweetened to wine   bloody as house
geraniums   in a windy rage they were already
fallen   curled into dry claws   gone from themselves

and we were worn out with friends who'd traveled
three hundred miles because of their love of leaves
which they admired more than anything else
in nature   as for apples   they reminded us that
thousands were being piled at this very moment
into the fruit stalls of the Korean markets
of our old city

Connections: Vermont   Vietnam (I)

Hot summer day
on the River Road
swimmers of the Ompompanoosuc
dust in my eyes
        oh
        it is the hot wind from Laos
        the girl in Nhe An covers her face with a straw hat
        as we pass   she breathes   through cloth
        she stands between two piles of stone

        the dust of National Highway 1 blinds

me
summertime
I drive through Vermont
my fist on the horn, barefoot
        like Ching

Connections: Vermont   Vietnam (II)

The generals came to the President
We are the laughingstock of the world
What world? he said
                    the world
                    the world

Vermont
    the green world
    the green mountain

Across the valley
someone is clearing a field
he is making a tan rectangle
he has cut a tan rectangle on Lyme Hill
the dark wood
the deposed farm
                    the mist is sipped up by the sun
                    the mist is eaten by the sun

What world?   he said

What mountain?   said the twenty ships of the Seventh Fleet
rolling on the warm waves   lobbing shells all the summer day
into green distance

        on Trung Son mountain Phan Su told a joke:
        The mountain is torn, the trees are broken
        how easy it is to gather wood
        to repair my house in the village which is broken by bombs

His shirt is plum-colored, is brown like dark plums
the sails on the sampans that fish in the sea of the Seventh Fleet
                    are plum-colored

the holes in the mountain are red
the earth of that province is red   red
                                        world

IV

Song Stanzas of Private Luck

To Be Added to Sometimes
and Sometimes to Be Subtracted From
As Events Prove One More Wrong than Right

Oh the year before I was born
        the sanitary napkin was invented
        the sanitary napkin
        the sanitary napkin
Nearly as important as the diaphragm
        more important
        for the girl child's first life
the cleanliness   the sweetness
        the excellent blood-consuming
        sanitary napkin

(And in parenthesis   according
to *The New York Times*   in my sixty-fifth year
the women of Eritrea were freed
        to enter the legislature
        and the trenches
this was because a sanitary napkin factory
        had been established
        a state enterprise with
entrepreneurial intentions as remarkable as capitalism)

Oh the year I was born
        the Joint Distribution Committee
        the famous   now hardly known at all
        Joint Distribution Committee
traveled to Russia to save Jewish orphans
of which there were many
        though years later

more   more   more
were made in another country and fewer were saved

Oh the year before I was born
        my mother and my father and
        my grandmother called Babashka
had already been in the U.S. for seventeen years
        and had missed civil war
        revolution and the terrible pogroms
        of Kishinev   Berditchev
they had been present for the pogrom of 1905   in which
our Rusya   our brother our uncle waving the workers' flag
        was murdered   the serious
        high-flying   bright red
        heavy   wind-enchanted
        workers' flag

Oh but in the very year I was born
        our uncle Grisha was sent away
        was shipped away from home
        to die in his own old country
brand-new Russia   oh the year that I was born
        no one told me any of this
        none of the above was mentioned
the word deportation was not said
        the word anarchist
        the word Palmer raid
the year that I was born was never spoken of
as the year of exile   of lifelong sorrow
that year was never mentioned to me
        by my father or my mother

except to say
ah   have we already told you how
        we were longing for you
        in our middle age
        after repeated requests

with the others almost grown
one winter day and your father in
sleepy attendance in one of the
office rooms downstairs   and everyone else
waiting in the hall   into our household
of secrecy
silence and jokes
you were finally born

Some Nearly Songs

The Old Dog's Song

Where can I shit
         said the old dog
turning this way and that
the grasses are gone
         the asphalt is slimy with oil
on the nice rubbly lots
         there are six-story buildings
where can I shit
         said the old dog
         turning this way and that

Where can I turn
         said the old dog
no one is in heat
         on this block at least
my old friends have altered
    or snap   they show me their teeth
         not their ass
         said the old dog
turning this way and that

This leash is so loose
         said the old dog
turning this way and that
nobody cares if I run
         the children have gone
the man who hangs on is like me
he looks up the block and then down
         turning this way and that
said the old dog
         turning this way and that

34th Street Song

With joy she showed the traveler Macy's
That's Macy's there   right by Korvette's
                        and Gimbel's

Oh you were right not to get out at 14th Street
Macy's is nice   but Klein's was the store
                        and it ended

The Sad Children's Song

This house is a wreck said the children
when they came home with their children
Your papers are all over the place
The chairs are covered with books
and look   brown leaves are piled on the floor
under the wandering Jews

Your face is a wreck said the children
when they came home with their children
There are lines all over your face
your neck's like a curious turtle's
Why did you let yourself go?
Where are you going without us?

This world is a wreck said the children
when they came home with their children
There are bombs all over the place
There's no water   the fields are all poisoned
Why did you leave things like this?
Where can we go said the children
What can we say to our children?

Traveler

He travels three hundred miles to New York
carrying the works of Kawabata
when he returns they return with him

What are they doing in his suitcase all that time

Speaking to one another as the books of any author will do
arguing the past and future of technical authority
ghosts invented for melody's sake   it's the tune
the time sings   all our stories are set to it

Sitting in the bus   watching New England curl
around its rivers   thinking of his own long
difficult novel   he will place *The Sound
of the Mountain* on his lap   he will ask
its intelligent advice

Speaker and Speaker

Standing in high grass at home imagining farm
   and granary   he looks east
         he praises Him
         astonished
and last night as we returned from our long walk
across Luquillo Beach we saw the colorless sun fall
between dark rain and the flashing sea
                    I think he praised Him
white birds flew up against the night
But for everyday life, he shows no gratitude

Still his courage is greater than mine
Days pass   no voice answers his
              My dear   I say
this is because the times are bad
speaker and speaker do not know one another
and the song sung by the people to the singer
is not known
          though the melody is theirs

Quarrel

Bob and I
    in different rooms
    talking to ourselves
carrying on
    last night's
    hard conversation
convinced
    the other one
    the life companion
    wasn't listening

Autumn

1

What is sometimes called a
    tongue of flame
or an arm extended burning
    is only the long
red and orange branch of
    a green maple
in early September   reaching
    into the greenest field
out of the green woods   at the
    edge of which the birch trees
appear a little tattered   tired
    of sustaining delicacy
all through the hot summer   re-
    minding everyone (in
our family) of a Russian
    song   a story
by Chekhov   or my father

2

What is sometimes called a
    tongue of flame
or an arm extended   burning
    is only the long
red and orange branch of
    a green maple
in early September   reaching
    into the greenest field
out of the green woods   at the
    edge of which the birch trees

appear a little tattered   tired
    of sustaining delicacy
all through the hot summer   re-
    minding everyone (in
our family) of a Russian
    song   a story by
Chekhov or my father on
    his own lawn   standing
beside his own wood in
    the United States of
America   saying (in Russian)
    this birch is a lovely
tree   but among the others
    somehow superficial

South Window

Man peeing
        by the woodpile
in the rain
        sky-blue   bird-blue
poncho

my man
        sometimes
more often
        his own

Man walking into
        deep woods
dark green leaves
        splashing
blue plastic

summer mist
        on hot earth
breathing him
        away

My Father at 85

My father said
        how will they get out of it
        they're sorry they got in

My father says
        how will they get out
        Nixon   Johnson   the whole bunch
        they don't know how

Goddamn it he says
        I'd give anything to see it
        they went in over their heads

He says
        greed   greed   time
        nothing is happening fast enough

My Father at 89

His brain simplified itself
saddening everyone   but he
asked us   children
don't you remember my dog Mars
who met me on the road
when I came home   lonesome
and singing   walking
from the Czar's prison

One Day I Decided

One day I decided to not grow any older
lots of luck I said to myself
(my joking self)   then I looked up at the sky
which is wide   its blueness   its whiteness

low on my left   the steamy sun rose   moved

I placed my hand against it   my whole hand
which is broad from pinky to thumb   no   my
two hands   I bared my teeth to it   my teeth
are strong   secure on their gold posts   I breathed
deeply   I held my breath   I stood on my toes   ah

then I was taller   still the clouds sailed
through me   around me   it's true   I'm just
like them   summertime water that the sun
sips and spits into this guzzling earth

In Aix

The doves   the speckled doves
are cooing in French   in high
female French   the shutters
clatter against their latches

The rain is the rain of Aix a-
wash in old paintings of
marsh and mist by Granet   the rain
splashes the shutters the rain is

bathed in the clouds of Chernobyl
last night on the evening
news we heard how nightingales
blowing north from Poland
folded their wings   fell over
the border and died in Germany

On the Ramblas
A Tree   A Girl

Anyone would love to paint from memory
the bark of a plane tree in Barcelona
little geographies of burgundy turn to olive
before your very eyes or peel to that yellow
the pale cream of all the apartment rooms
in the Bronx

or write one proper grieving song for the girl
beautiful but burned in face and arm
smoke smeared into lifelong recognition
screaming in Catalan at the man who stands
before her   who supplicates   whose hands
brought together in supplication
beg   for what
        pimp   lover   father?

I say father because I'm old
and know how we beg the young to live
no matter what

Oh

Oh, the dreamer said
and dreamed himself she

it was an unusual day
when all the suns stood
visible and we could see
our light small sighted sun

its rays were bones
of the old wars

In France

Poor talker   mouthperson
   alone
waiting for bravery

the muse (in
   other words)
     Oh language

circumvent my tongue
   tell pen
     Move!

Make text

I Gave Away That Kid

I gave away that kid like he was an old button
    Here old button get off of me
    I don't need you anymore
    go on   get out of here
    go into the army
    sew yourself onto the colonel's shirt
    or the captain's fly   jackass
    don't you have any sense
    don't you read the papers
    why are you leaving now?

That kid walked out of here like he was the cat's pajamas
    what are you wearing pj's for   you damn fool?
    why are you crying   you couldn't
    get another job anywhere anyways
    go march to the army's drummer
    be a man like all your dead uncles
    then think of something else to do

Lost him, sorry about that   the President said
    he was a good boy
    never see one like him again
    Why don't you repeat that   your honor
    why don't you sizzle up the meaning
    of that sentence for your breakfast
    why don't you stick him in a prayer
    and count to ten before my wife gets you

That boy is a puddle in Beirut   the paper says
    scraped up for singing in church
    too bad   too bad is a terrible tune
    it's no song at all   how come you sing it?

I gave away that kid like he was an old button
	Here old button get offa me
	I don't need you anymore
	go on get out of here
	go into the army
	sew yourself onto the colonel's shirt
	or the captain's fly jackass
	don't you have any sense
	don't you read the papers
	why are you leaving now?

Subway Station

The child is speaking to the father
he is looking into the father's eyes
The father doesn't answer
The child is speaking Vietnamese
The father doesn't answer
The child is speaking English
The father doesn't answer
The father is staring at a mosaic in blue and green
and lavender   three small ships in harbor
set again and again in the white tiled
beautiful   old   unrenovated subway
station   Clark Street   Brooklyn

Bridges

Along the beach beyond La Boca   the Luquillo River
stretches and bends to reach the sea   in tropical
easiness it takes no trouble   at high tide the ad-
venturous sea pours salt into the eyes of the
sweet water fish

Clouds blow and darken toward the mists of the
rain forest mountain   sun falls from the aging
day and looks at night   but first it shines the
palm leaves   blinding the lizards

Fifty feet toward sunset the river widens   it was
once two rivers   I can see the far glint of a steel
bridge   cars moving fast on Route 3

A dark form stands in the Luquillo River   an old bridge
pillar and planks rotted   unconnected to either shore

Long ago in morning shadow this bridge rattled the
campesinos and the pescadores in their carts hurrying
to Fajardo   they traveled in sight of the fishy
noisy sea

*There were four bridges over the river near Nien Trach
south south of Tonkin Bay   north of Quanghbinh   three
were splintered and burned   torn from their village
shores   one stood   a dike of mud and rocks as wide
as a small truck*

We drive to the airport near San Juan   the sea on one hand
the darkening river   the old unconnected bridge   a platform
on mossy stilts   the traffic is heavy on Route 3   called by
American Army Engineers the Road of the Sixty-fifth Infantry

In Hanoi   1969

Sometimes
on this green hill
I walk around all day
in my cotton shirt and shiny black pajama pants
the rubber tire sandals
that I bought in the Foreigners' Store

The tailor was tired of pleasing Russians
He looked Tuan in the eye and said   an American?
what is the Fatherland Front thinking of now?
there is no cotton   there is very little cotton

He measured carefully   Linda and I were ashamed
to be American and fat   the Russian woman laughed at us
she watched   the tailor said   choose your material   there
are the bolts of cloth   he was disgusted
He said   take anything   what is it worth   this
is the Foreigners' Store   Tuan told us later
he suffers   he is an intelligent man

Then I spoke Russian   the language
my childhood had casually stored   tell me madame
I don't sew   which is the proper material?

She answered   my dear   that is beautiful   and that too
is good   but that!   only the Vietnamese
would wear   she was nicely dressed
a diplomat's wife   she will travel   she
will buy lovely saris in Delhi   and in North Africa
a djellaba of fine wool   a proud and visiting life
is before her   she will be with her husband an empire's
interested emissary to the quiet edge
of the terrible wars

Two Villages

In Duc Ninh a village of 1,654 households
over 100 tons of rice and cassava were burned
18,138 cubic meters of dike were destroyed
There were 1,077 air attacks
There is a bomb crater that measures 150 feet across
It is 50 feet deep

Mr. Tat said: The land is more exhausted than the people
I mean to say that the poor earth
is tossed about
thrown into the air again and again
it knows no rest

whereas the people have dug tunnels
and trenches   they are able in this way
to lead normal family lives

In Trung Trach
a village of 850 households
a chart is hung in the House of Tradition

rockets   522
attacks   1,201
big bombs   6,998
napalm   1,383
time bombs   267
shells   12,291
pellet bombs   2,213

Mr. Tuong of the Fatherland Front
has a little book
In it he keeps the facts
carefully added

That Country

This is about the women of that country
Sometimes they spoke in slogans
They said
> We patch the roads as we patch our sweetheart's trousers
> The heart will stop but not the transport
They said
> We have ensured production even near bomb craters
> Children let your voices sing higher than the explosions
>   of the bombs
They said
> We have important tasks to teach the children
> that the people are the collective masters
> to bear hardship
> to instill love in the family
> to guide the good health of the children (they must
> wear clothing according to climate)
They said
> Once men beat their wives
> now they may not
> Once a poor family sold its daughter to a rich old man
> now the young may love one another
They said
> Once we planted our rice any old way
> now we plant the young shoots in straight rows
> so the imperialist pilot can see how steady our
> hands are

In the evening we walked along the shores of the Lake
                                     of the Restored Sword

I said   is it true?   we are sisters?
They said   Yes, we are of one family

Street Corner Dialogue

Thank God for the old Jewish ladies
    though their sons are splendid with houses
    and brilliant from college
    they take our leaflets

Sometimes they say
    Pishers   what's on your mind
    don't get excited   Hitler is
    dead   where are the sweatshops

Then we say   Missus
    did you forget Vietnam
    I won't speak about Israel   turn
    around maybe 80° you'll see a few
    sweatshops   not to mention
    imperialism's furnace   the nation
    of Africa

They answer   Of course
    oh yes   as usual   we heard it
    before   naturally   oy   the poor
    people are dying   dying   dying
    foolish girl   listen   you'll never
    stop it   the dying from killing

Then we tell them only five words
    So   why did you live?

Uh-oh   a fresh mouth   but
    darling you're right   in your life
    you shouldn't give up the ship   so long
    you got strength   maybe this world
    wouldn't turn out a total disaster

Illegal Aliens

The Chicago airport
O'Hare
4:30 a.m.

fifty men
in double lines
handcuffed

dark men

probably Mexicans
wearing
the work clothes

in which they were taken

brightness of the airport
the empty shopping stalls blaze

a tall sandy-haired man
leads them   not in uniform
gray pants   an ordinary
windbreaker   he calls
aquí aquí   waving his hands

a young woman in the rear
shouts   go on now
aquí aquí you got to
go the way he says

In San Salvador (I)

Come   look   they said
here are the photograph albums
these are our children

We are called The Mothers of the Disappeared
we are also the mothers of those who were seen once more
and then photographed   sometimes parts of them
could not be found

a breast   an eye   an arm is missing
sometimes a whole stomach
that is why we are called   The Mothers
of the Disappeared   although we have these large
heavy photograph albums full of beautiful
torn faces

In San Salvador (II)

Then one woman spoke   About my son
she said   I want to tell you   This
is what happened

                I heard a cry   Mother
Mother   keep the door closed   a scream
the high voice of my son   his scream
jumped into my belly   his voice
boiled there and boiled until hot water
ran down my thigh

                The following week I waited
by the fire making tortilla   I heard   what?
the voice of my second son   Mother   quickly
turn your back to the door   turn your back
to the window

                And one day of the third week
my third son called me   oh Mother   please
hurry up   hold out your apron   they are
stealing my eyes

                And then in the fourth week   my
fourth son   No

        No   it was morning   he stood
in the doorway   he was taken right
there   before my eyes the parts of
the body of my son were tormented   are
you listening?   do you understand
this story?   there was only one
child   one boy   like Mary I had
only one son

For Mike and Jeannie: Resisters
Fifteen Years Later

The car turned over three times
rolled down the nice
summertime hayfield

at the riverbank   The boy
hung upside down in his seat belt
glass   glittering dust
        in his hair   on his long lashes
        gently we brushed his bloody lips
        Did I live?   he asked

Then Mike said   Look!   sometimes
        what you see   you see your own death

I want to know
who saw you Mike   with Jeannie
on that Virginia road   six months later
        tilting   tilting into the
        rain-softened shoulder   over
        over   down   flung
from that tin can of a car

did one of you see the other
dead   did one of you say
No   No   Us?

Learning from Barbara Deming

First: She's a listener.
So you can learn something about paying attention.

Second: She's stubborn.
So you can learn how to stand, look into the other's
    face and not run.

Third: She's just.
So you can learn something about patience.

Fourth: She loves us—women I mean—and speaks to
    the world.
So you can learn how to love women and men.

Happiness

If you have acquired a taste for happiness
        it's very hard to do without
so you try jollity for a while
jokes
        and
                merriment

Song is one of the famous methods
for continuing or entrenching happiness

You may say   what
about sex   is it its own
keen pleasure or according to some
        the night's sorrow

Here is another example of ordinary joy
it is prose   but uses whole days and nights
        the gathering together of comrades
        in bitter disagreement   then resolution
        followed by determined action

Still   the face of life will change
partly because of those miserable scratches it makes
on its own aging surface
        then
        happiness
in the risky busy labor of Repair the World
after which   for the unsated   there will surely be
talking all night   dances in schoolrooms and kitchens
        and later
        love
of happiness   the most famous of all

Definition

My dissent is cheer
a thankless disposition
first as the morning star
    my ambition: good luck

and why not   a flight
over the wide dilemma
and then good night to
    sad forever

Age

Frightened   fearful   afraid
    older   waking in fear
healthy   feet okay   appetite
    only teeth half gone   wrists
strong   night love   waking in
    fear   older   old   nothing
ahead   glad to say ah!
    willing   working   tired
laugh!   dance after supper
    knees useful   love   waking
afraid   bad news   friends old
    sickness   becoming well
an occupation a
    hope against age   fear

Love

Handsome men wearing red ties walk past my window
not one but three   this morning!   their coats open
their ties flying   as though spring had made some
deliberate move on our street   maybe a fur-tipped
bud among the hedges   a fact   years and
years ago I saw you pass   your face rosy from that
interior lifelong commotion   your head forward
stubborn against a March wind   day after day
for nearly a month   as you walked with con-
siderable eagerness toward your daily life
right past my window   I thought   who
is that man   then I thought   oh
I already know him

Time

Now time himself   the master streamer
grew
by pools and ponds
then strenuously   to accommodate the generations
became a sea

in which the fish and thee
my love   by dark and night light swim
and nations drown

The Women's Prison: El Salvador
The Ballad of Visiting Day

In Ilopongo Prison
    a girl is sitting quietly
She has only one leg   she
    wears a pretty dress and

her hair is done in braids
    her mother sits beside her
wearing a black dress   her brother
    whistles through two reeds

and watches the sad women
    In Ilopongo Prison
a little prisoner calls out   María
    come talk to the North Americans

This prisoner has been a woman
    only a short time   she
wears a black beret   she wears
    a sash   she is a commandante

she fought away from girlhood
    in the high mountains of her country
Come come and tell your story
    to the North American women

about your brother Jaime
    martyred while still
a schoolboy   the mother hears
    his name Jaime   Jaime called

out loud   with her hand she brushes
        the dress all full of flowers
that she brought her daughter with one leg

        she sighs   she sighs deeply
you would think her body was
        a drum of thumping air

I stood inside our garden
        where we planted beans
the beans were climbing high
        five men came and whispered

—oh we are Jaime's friends
        oh how we long to see him
we knew him in the hills
        the little bumpy hills

that stumbled into mountains
        he said he had a sister
just like a morning rose
        that's how we recognized you

Tell us María   rosy beauty
        where is your brother Jaime
he's our brother too
        our comrade

I don't know where he is
        Come now little sister
you must tell us   we lack
        all happiness without him

(There were five men)   believe me
        the last time that I saw him
those were the days of rain
        You stupid girl   you're lying

You're lying   liar tell us   we'll burn
        your mother's house   we are
the Guard   now tell us   then
        one man raised his rifle   why?
I cried out   why?   Lightning
        slapped the earth beside me

All round the prison floor
        the little babies crawled
The mother looked at them
        she smoothed her daughter's dress

(the dress so full of flowers)
        Thank Mary   blessed virgin
that we were spared such shame
        The little commandante

cried out   no shame no shame
        she banged the table hard
no shame   these children are not
        the first whose fathers are unknown

We are the babes of rape
        said the little commandante
our villages were torn   our mothers
        violated   our fathers split in two

Still we have named our struggle
        for Farabundo Martí and we are
fierce and restless till justice and
        the land belong to the poor people

In Ilopongo Prison
        a girl is sitting quietly
she has only one leg   her mother
        sits beside her brushing
her long hair   her brother

          watches   whistles through two reeds
the little commandante talks
          with the North American women
the babies crying crawl toward
          the breasts of their lonesome mothers

The Dance in Jinotega

In Jinotega women greeted us
with thousands of flowers   roses
it was hard to tell   the petals
on our faces and arms   falling

then embraces and the Spanish language
which is a little like a descent of
petals   pink   and orange

Suddenly out of the hallway   our
gathering place   AMNLAE   the
Asociación de Mujeres   women
came running   seat yourselves dear
guests from the north   we announce
a play   a dance   a play   the women
their faces mountain river Indian
European   Spanish   dark-haired
women

            dance in gray-green
fatigues   they dance   the Contra who
circles the village waiting
for the young teacher   the health worker
(these are the strategies)   the farmer
in the high village walks out into the
morning toward the front which is a
circle of terror

            they dance
the work of women and men   they dance
the plowing of the fields   they kneel
to the harrowing with the machetes   they
dance the sowing of seed (which is always

a dance) and the ripening of corn   the
flowers of grain   they dance the harvest
they raise their machetes for
the harvest   the machetes are high
                    but no!

out of the hallway in green and gray
come those who dance the stealth
of the Contra   cruelly they
dance the ambush   the slaughter of
the farmer   they are the death dancers
who found the schoolteacher   they caught
the boy who   dancing   brought seeds in
his hat all the way from Matagalpa   they
dance the death of the mother   the
father   the rape of the daughter   they
dance the child murdered   the seeds
spilled and trampled   they dance
sorrow   sorrow

                    they dance the
search for the Contra and the defeat
they dance a comic dance   they make a
joke of the puppetry of the Contra of
Uncle Sam who is the handler of puppets
they dance rage and revenge   they place
the dead child (the real sleeping baby)
on two chairs   which is the bier for
the little actor   they dance prayer
bereavement   sorrow   they mourn

Is there applause for such theater?

Silence   then   come let us dance
together now you know   the usual
dance of couples Spanish or North
American   let us dance in twos and

threes   let us make little circles   let us
dance as though at a festival or in peace-
time together and alone   whirling   stamping
our feet   bowing to one another

                    the children
gather petals from the floor to throw
at our knees   we dance   the children
too banging into us   into each other and
one small boy dances alone   pulling
at our skirts   wait   he screams   stop!
he tugs at the strap of our camera   Stop!
stop dancing   I'm Carlos   take a picture
of me   No!   Now!   Right now!   because
soon   Look!   See Pepe!   even tomorrow
I could be dead like him

                    the music
catches its breath   the music
jumping in the guitar and phonograph holds
still and waits   no no   we say   Carlos
not you   we put our fingers on his little
shoulder   we touch his hair   but one of
us is afraid   for god's sake take his
picture   so we lift him up   we photo-
graph him   we pass him from one to
another   we photograph him again and
again   with each of us crying or
laughing with him in our arms
we dance

People in My Family

In my family
people who were eighty-two were very different
from people who were ninety-two

The eighty-two-year-old people grew up
  it was 1914
  this is what they knew
  War World War War

That's why when they speak to the child
they say
  poor little one . . .

The ninety-two-year-old people remember
  it was the year 1905
  they went to prison
  they went into exile
  they said ah soon

When they speak to the grandchild
they say
  yes there will be revolution
  then there will be revolution then
  once more then the earth itself
  will turn and turn and cry out oh I
  have been made sick

    then you my little bud
    must flower and save it

In the Bus

Somewhere between Greenfield and Holyoke
snow became rain
and a child passed through me
as a person moves through mist
as the moon moves through
a dense cloud at night
as though I were cloud or mist
a child passed through me

On the highway that lies
across miles of stubble
and tobacco barns our bus speeding
speeding disordered the slanty rain
and a girl with no name   naked
wearing the last nakedness of
childhood   breathed in me
                    once   no
                    two breaths
a sigh   she whispered   Hey you
begin again
                    Again?
again   again   you'll see
it's easy   begin again   long ago

House: Some Instructions

If you have a house
you must think about it all the time
as you reside in the house so
it must be a home in your mind

you must ask yourself (wherever you are)
have I closed the front door

and the back door is often forgotten
not against thieves necessarily

but the wind   oh   if it blows
either door open   then the heat

the heat you've carefully nurtured
with layers of dry hardwood

and a couple of opposing green
brought in to slow the fire

as well as the little pilot light
in the convenient gas backup

all of that care will be mocked because
you have not kept the house on your mind

but these may actually be among
the smallest concerns   for instance

the house could be settling   you may
notice the thin slanting line of light

above the doors   you have to think about that
luckily you have been paying attention

the house's dryness can be humidified
with vaporizers in each room and pots

of water on the woodstove   should you leave
for the movies after dinner   ask yourself

have I turned down the thermometer
and moved all wood paper away from the stove

the fiery result of excited distraction
could be too horrible to describe

now we should talk especially to Northerners
of the freezing of the pipe   this can often

be prevented by pumping water continuously
through the baseboard heating system

allowing the faucet to drip drip continuously
day and night   you must think about the drains

separately   in fact you should have established
their essential contribution to the ordinary

kitchen and toilet life of the house
digging these drains deep into warm earth

if it hasn't snowed by mid-December you
must cover them with hay   sometimes rugs

and blankets have been used   do not be
troubled by their monetary value

as this is a regionally appreciated emergency
you may tell your friends to consider

your house as their own   that is
if they do not wear outdoor shoes

when thumping across the gleam of their poly-
urethaned floors they must bring socks or slippers

to your house as well   you must think
of your house when you're in it and

when you're visiting the superior cabinets
and closets of others   when you approach

your house in the late afternoon
in any weather   green or white   you will catch

sight first of its new aluminum snow-resistant
roof and the reflections in the cracked windows

its need in the last twenty-five years for paint
which has created a lovely design

in russet pink and brown   the colors of un-
intentioned neglect   you must admire the way it does *not*

(because of someone's excellent decision
sixty years ago) stand on the high ridge deforming

the green profile of the hill but rests in the modesty
of late middle age under the brow of the hill with

its back to the dark hemlock forest looking steadily
out for miles toward the cloud refiguring meadows and

mountains of the next state   coming up the road
by foot or auto the house can be addressed personally

House!   in the excitement of work and travel to
other people's houses with their interesting improvements

we thought of you often and spoke of your coziness
in winter   your courage in wind and fire   your small

airy rooms in humid summer   how you nestle in spring
into the leaves and flowers of the hawthorn and the sage green

leaves of the Russian olive tree   House!   you were not forgotten

VI

*Begin
Again*

The Immigrant Story

One day in my family's life
I entered the English language
d's and *t*'s in my teeth   *s*'s steaming

I elongated *i*'s
lost a few *r*'s   included
them where they weren't wanted

I often stationed a preposition
at the end of a sentence
this was to guard against
aggrieved inflection

Much to my surprise strangers understood me
I continued talking   I was brazen   I said

everywhere I go there are verbs that are doing nothing
it has been years since certain nouns were referred to
            by their right names
I must ask a sad question
will the laws of entropy operate in spite of strictness
is there a literature that chants the disappearance
            of tongues

Translation

I was reading *The English Patient* by
Michael Ondaatje and saw in one sentence
the name Savonarola   oh   I was over-
turned   tumbled into the downstairs music parlor
my own shouting place   where I roared his biblical
rage in King James English   then listened
at our player's rowdiest volume to the *Passion*
of St. Matthew   singing   singing that German
into my skull for future resonance

In those years my European cousins   before the arrival
of gas fire strangulation or only lifelong despair
had begun to wonder how they could ever have spoken for
love of literature or childhood's language a sentence
by Rilke or Hölderlin or even Kafka

As for me my ear has the normal trouble of an American
speaker of foreign tongues   still when I'm walking along
the path between our river and the railroad bed   the
hundred closed cars of the New York to Quebec freight will
slow from thunder to that heavy thud which I cannot
help but translate as it passes our innocent and
ignorant village into German

Signs

A man hung a sign above the town
it said   suffering   in small letters
meaning (I thought) modest suffering

This made another man angry   he
had a sign printed in large letters
it said HOPE   meaning (I thought)
immodest hope

Then acres of coffee or cocoa were laid
like foreign weather on fields of maize
and rice   under the sun the desert waited

The Woman Says

The woman says   read me
she puts a finger to the corner of her mouth
no smiles
the woman stands on our stoop
she screams   what?   language
she wants to shake her father out
of her mother's flesh
this has been one of her worries

I know something else
she drummed her children out
the broken door of her life
they were too old anyway (she said)

Who am I to speak
I live my life in the blind box of sanity
I want to befriend her
in the days of tell all
she told all
that's what I wanted to hear

Faces

A man my age
wanted to talk

to the owner of
the hardware store

he said good morning
mister   their faces looked

at one another   no   no
their eyes   oh no

their eyes never met
only their faces   one

young   one old   I have
a great new line this season

the young face said   that so?
I don't need it any-

ways   the old face
said   turning   turning

It's True

Everywhere people love their children
even the father at the railroad station
in Windsor Connecticut
who will appear tomorrow in the morning paper
in drunken sorrow having beaten his baby
to the gasping edge of life

he stands this early afternoon
holding the child in his arms   telling her
between kisses   here comes the big train
listen to the whistle   and now look   look
the lady in that window she sees how beautiful
you are   she's waving to us

Tenth Grade

On the deep snowy field
behind the school   in
six-foot letters he
shoveled the words I
WAS HERE

Who?   I

the one who cried   despaired
raged   smiled   staring at
the vast winter meadow   the
white snow   white

I

The Boy   His Mother

                    she said
you were a wonderful boy this evening
at dinner among friends   so attentive   so
grown-up   the boy's heart   oh his ribs
may crack with happiness   he runs dangerously
out into the street   calling   come come every-
body it's this way   we're going this way   he turns
wants to look up into her face   come Mother   she
laughs and follows   but there's no help   his eyes
are tipped with tears

                    in only
a few birthdays love will find his whole body
beat at his skin to get out   out   his knees
weakened   he bows his head   kneels
before the other   a girl   love-threaded
as he has been   begging relief

Suppertime

The father asks for salt
three women rise   the mother
the grandmother   the aunt   there
is only one salt shaker   what
can be done

The child continues to eat   she
is interested in the problem
each day a different woman wins
the child is relieved   she will not
have to choose which one to defend
which one to oppose   which one to love

How to Tell a Story
(My Method)   (Most of the Time)

Now prose

Find the paragraph to
hold the poem steady
for six or eight pages

the teller is waiting
her voice   her throat
is still narrow   help
help   she'd cry if she could

she may be frightened by
those arts   invention and
memory   solitude's heat

what is her language   try to
assemble her mother's
whispers   her father's way
of lifting a sentence
then silencing it   which
of the world's years freed them
to speak to strangers   why
are they laughing

don't let her lose the poem
in the telling of day by
day   because the subject
is time   the place is only
paper   the story is still
a puzzle   the teller
knows why

The Word Thrum

is a wonderful word
I've tried but haven't been able to use it
it sounded itself to me in a poem by Jane Cooper
    I now live among trees   their branches
    twigs and leaves   a gentle wind blows
but the word thrum has come to me too late

My Father Said

Why not my father said   so
you'll be like them   pointing
to all the aunts as round as
city water barrels   laughing
no disgust or disapproval
only prophecy

for instance   your aunt Esfere
eighteen   just off the boat   needed
a corset   ashamed   she didn't know
the custom   your mother said   go
Zenya   measure   put your arms around
her middle but bring a string for where
your hands don't meet   well soon

she was married   dear girl what
can you do   you're made the same
maybe a little lighter   like
your mama   listen to me   once
once long ago   in times cold like
ice   like iron   such softness
that's why we loved our wives

He Wanders

if this continues the children
may take him into their care
(lovingly) or hire a stranger
with an American accent

he explains   he must go back
to a place he never saw before
he may have to go tomorrow
this is a mystery

the police will bring him home   they
are not like the hooligans in
that old country   still they are not
hospitable

he waited patiently at the
officer's desk   he was not offered
even one small glass of vodka
the children don't know what to do

the grandchildren say   grandpa
that's okay   come and go   why not
come sometimes and sometimes go

Four Short Pieces

What did the poem say that day
we were talking   talking
it said   be quiet   give me
the last word   without it
you've hardly a thought

                    At that time
                    I had a pocketful
                    of excellent stones

                    but I was not
                    without sin   what
                    could I do but
                    walk heavily   heavily

One day I couldn't take a joke anymore
I could make one as easy as ever
but wondered why the listener would laugh
weren't things as bad for her
as for the rest of the world?

                    Life is two dreams
                    yours and your beloved's
                    at breakfast   laboring to listen
                    suffering to tell   someone
                    cries   who made the coffee
                    and all is lost

The Poet's Occasional Alternative

I was going to write a poem
I made a pie instead   it took
about the same amount of time
of course the pie was a final
draft   a poem would have had some
distance to go   days and weeks and
much crumpled paper

the pie already had a talking
tumbling audience among small
trucks and a fire engine on
the kitchen floor

everybody will like this pie
it will have apples and cranberries
dried apricots in it   many friends
will say   why in the world did you
make only one

this does not happen with poems

because of unreportable
sadnesses I decided to
settle this morning for a re-
sponsive eatership   I do not
want to wait a week   a year   a
generation for the right
consumer to come along

One of the Softer Sorrows of Age

I asked
did this happen before you moved to New York or
just after you rented the house   the one that
was once a shed   it did look nice finally   or
was it afterwards   when you found that great old farmhouse
way out of the village on the dirt road   when was it . . .

She answered
why do you talk like that   everybody is forgetful
what are you trying to prove

my dear girl   I AM growing old

oh ma   ma . . .

✯

When this old body
finds that old body
what a nice day it is

when that old body
loves this old body
it's dreamless to sleep
and busy to wake up

when this old body says
you're a little lumpy here and there
but you're the same old body after all

old body   old body   in which somewhere
between crooked toe and forgetful head
the flesh encounters soul
and whispers   you

When I Was Asked
How I Could Leave Vermont
in the Middle of October

I did not want to be dependent on autumn
I wanted to miss it for once   drop into
another latitude where it wasn't so
well known   I wanted to show that beauty
can be held in the breath just as we breathe
grief and betrayal   they don't always
have to be happening in the living minute

Look   there it is now   our own golden
wine-colored world-famous Vermont fall   green
as summer to begin with and then the sunny
morning draws mist out of the cold night river
the maples are sweetened   there's a certain
skipped beat   a scalding   as you live that
loyal countryside   ablaze   trembling
toward its long winter   nobody should have
to bear all that death-determined beauty
every single year   this aging body knows
it can't be borne

Weather

This year   the fourth without snow
the earth is like iron   spiky grasses
stand in the dangerous yard

listen   a front is coming   earth
doesn't care   its jagged face is
frozen   but look   the trees are wild
with caring   whipped by the wind
whipper of trees   scatterer and
shatterer of birds

this is a front   defined by
racing cloud after long stillness
and wind roars in the pines   the pines
roar   here comes weather   riding
its back   the cold then colder lies
down on the iron ground   ice hums

Three days after writing the final draft of this poem the snow began. By morning it had blown into roadside drifts, stopped, a week of flurries, then snow again, fine skiing even in the woods, a couple of days of flurries, then a two-foot snow covering ski trails, roads, doorways, then snow, a great winter of extraordinary snowfall, and here it is April and another four inches, the world black and white, except for the beech and oak leaves, a kind of domestic brown in the aristocratic woods.

In Montpelier, Vermont

In Montpelier this morning
all the men wear beards
this is wise in February

they are not wearing them for warmth
some are bald and hatless

many are going to a particular place
with address books in their hands
they are looking at the numbers above doors

others are just strolling down the sunny street
at 8 a.m. they heard the radio say

A GLORIOUS DAY! A GLORIOUS DAY!
there will be snow on all the hillsides
the roads are being plowed as we speak
it is cold as February must be
but our generous friend the sun
will be seen everywhere

Beef

In the long shadow of Mr. Clark's woods
Mr. Clark's twenty white-faced cows and their little
        white-faced calves
rest from their long day in the delectable pasture

Unlike their cousins in the dairy the calves have not
        been stolen
from the milk of their mothers (they often gambol about
as young farm animals do)

Above them the clouds are hurrying into a fat watery community
in the barnyard below   the pickup and the 'dozer
drive interestingly back and forth   behind them
the hemlock woods darken

NOW

I woke from a dream of verbs
 to the noise of modifiers
crackling around me

political modifiers probably
 restless
waiting for the wrong move

is this the dream of an old word person
 or the intervention of
reality   furious because
 of all that optimism
which was often gallant   useful
 in family life
fatal only to others

or is it because the time
 rose up on its hind legs
just as the air cleared   changed
 directions   took
all the maps in its teeth

could you have believed that this
 system of ours called capitalism
having chewed on all those poor
 nations and spit them out into
the back yard of the world's
 markets would then live
long enough to consume the earth
 and every generative
seed in its holy custody

what now?   in the journals
    of the indigenous people I've read
again and again   pay attention to
    the seventh generation and
to the sleeper to whom all is told

we are not accustomed
    to taking the advice of dreams
but I think we'd better not
    be so aloof   or resist
receiving information
    from our own godless
wintry darkness

Is There a Difference
Between Men and Women

Oh the slave trade
   the arms trade
death on the high seas
   massacre in the villages

       trade in the markets
          melons mustard greens
       cloth shining   dipped in
          onion dye beet grass
       trade in the markets   fish
          oil   yams   coconuts   leaves
     of water spinach   leaves
       of pure water   cucumbers
     pickled   walking back
       and forth along the stalls
     cloth bleached to ivory
       argument from stall to stall
     disgusted and delighted
       in the market

oh the worldwide arms trade
     the trade in women's bodies
the slave trade
   slaughter

       oranges coming in from
          the country in one
       basket on the long
          pole   coconuts in
       the other   on the
          shoulders of women

walking   knees slightly bent
scuffing   stumbling
along the road   bringing
rice into the city
hoisting the bundles of dry
mangrove for repair
of the household   trade
in the markets on
the women's backs and shoulders
yams   sometimes peanuts

oh the slave trade
the trade in the bodies of women
the worldwide unending arms trade
everywhere man-made slaughter

Reading the Newspapers
at the Village Store

this morning
    the hills rolled over
in mist   the hot
    watermaking sun
steamed into
    the tight wet elbows of
the valley   daily dutiful sun
    mocking my pessimism in
this world's year
    and one man spoke

cyclones earthquakes landslides floods
    what nature doesn't do
to those poor countries in the
    places where those people live
and look at this   aren't they
    always warring on each other
murdering and maiming one
    another without mercy?

the other man replied
    it was in the morning paper
a couple of months ago
    we came upon those very people
and slaughtered them from up high
    and maimed them in their hills
and valleys and their dry desert
    places   caught them morning and
night whether the sun was
    blessing or burning the green skin
off their farms outside

we caught them   those people
in their dangerous
    geographical places

No   No   the first man cried
    above them the sun as usual
stood still   the other man
    said   Ah!   then holding tight
to earth's thin coat   they fell
    toward night   the little death
of mild habitual murderers

The Desert Wasn't Loved
Enough   said Reich

It could have been the grassiest of places
wheat would have blown the thin air thick
with seed dust   trees would have stood
in natural patience throwing oxygen around
dropping leaves in compost gullies
making earth in sun and rotting shade

the deer and antelope after play would fuck
in the green evening   hills would fade in blues
and purples like remembered life
                                    but someone
came maybe with twenty goats   then later
with 30,000 cattle   then with teeth
of federal steel   or someone turned the river
backwards to nourish vacuum cleaners in the cities
and all these thousand miles of wetted fields dried
into sandy dust which no one can sweep up though
some who love will try

       Into the Arizona desert Wilhelm Reich
       came in a dune jeep made by Henry Ford
       he stepped out onto the pebbly sands
       he raised a mighty cactus up to God
         and cried   I love

What If (This Week)

What if this century doesn't end
what if the Serbs continue their snarling self-loving wrath
and the Kosovars their hopeless arming
and the Hutus their vengeful slaughtering rage
and the American armed mullahs of Afghanistan their devout
           exclusion of the joyful life of women
and the landowners of the world their terrible return again
           and again to what is unrightfully theirs
and the darker people burning with insult and pride
           of population
and the Americans their deliberate impoverishment of
           Vietnam in order to win the lost war
and the Russians continue their hard job of giving up old
           badness just to be bad like everyone else
and the Irish unstrung on the lyres of history
and the Somalis clanned and unclanned
and the Turks their habitual attacks on the Kurds
and the Iraqis their habitual attacks on the Kurds

What if my friend never stops saying   if I had six sons I'd
           give them all
what if I scream   horror
and she explains the idealistic politics of sacrificing sons

What if the thirty-six just men who repair the world year
           after year feel their frailty
and petition that One to increase their number
what if there is no answer from time-creating heaven
no sound   no interest   not a turning away   suddenly   absence
what if there is no child   male or female   white or black
           no mother   no child

This Life

My friend tells me
a man in my house jumped off the roof
the roof is the eighth floor of this building
the roof door was locked   how did he manage?
his girlfriend had said   goodbye I'm leaving
he was 22
his mother and father were hurrying
at that very moment
from upstate to help him move out of Brooklyn
they had heard about the girl

the people who usually look up
and call   jump jump   did not see him
the life savers who creep around the back staircases
and reach the roof's edge just in time
never got their chance   he meant it   he wanted
only one person to know

did he imagine that she would grieve
all her young life away   tell everyone
this boy I kind of lived with last year
he died on account of me

my friend was not interested   he said   you're always
inventing stuff   what I want to know   how could he throw
his life away   how do these guys do it
just like that   and here I am fighting this
ferocious insane vindictive virus day and
night   day and night   and for what?   for only
one thing   this life   this life

Sometimes

Sometimes you become
    sorry for someone
    a person dead

long ago   you think
    of him you
    are overcome

with sadness   so one day
    reading a book
    about a man

called Mr. Vasquez
    sorrow suddenly
    empowered me

I remembered
    my grandfather
    Asher

also a watchmaker
    like Mr. Vasquez
    in the story

and reading the
    precise faithful
    details of watch repair

I imagined my
    grandfather's life
    in the town

of Uzovka in
    Ukraine when
    it was common

for Jews (I learned)
    to be the re-
    pairers of clocks

and I felt his life
    as I never had
    before

though his photo-
    graph hung heavily
    in my grandmother's

room every day of
    my childhood
    the photograph

enlarged by the family
    Gutzeit   my own
    family (photography

also a Jewish
    trade) and I saw
    that young

bearded Jew
    on the wall
    above

my grandmother's
    bed and never
    sorrowed

for his fate until
    now   although my
    father at supper

told us (more than once)
    how my grandfather
    looking with love

and worry at my
   grandmother said
   ach Natasha

I am healthy now
   but I know I will
   die leaving you

an absolutely
   penniless widow
   with five young children

and that   my father said
   victoriously
   is just what he did

Leaflet

If you've noticed that people have been acting
    kind of nervous   think of whole nations
they are absolutely pathological
    one day we were selling them
so much killing hardware
    their governmental teeth
were eroding with the metallic grind
    but their appetites increased
along with our economic delight when
    we filled their commissaries
with our indigestible grain as well
    as other stuff they'd once
grown themselves   suddenly (it seemed
    to them) we stopped and declared
them enemies (for what we called
    geographically defensible
reasons) just when they considered us
    a safe source of appetite ful-
filling ordinance   without
    notice   even everyday fighter planes
were withheld   naturally they responded
    with infantile rage and alarming
violence   these countries
    have to be put away for their own
historic health   put out of their
    inflammable misery   embraced
properly by our embargoes   sanctions etc.
    it's a pity they act so crazy   look
how nervous you get when the weather changes

I See My Friend Everywhere

First she died   then on the bus
I saw her   my old friend dropped
her half fare into the slot
looked up   her eyes humorous
intelligent   cap of white hair
shining   I asked her   how's the boy
these days   not so good   but you
know that   your work?   is it going
well?   what work she whispered (bitterly
I thought)   are you all right?   why
do you ask?   I was afraid of her

the bus rocked and bumped over and
through New York   unsteady   I called out
STOP   this is where I get off   here?
since when?   oh for the last couple
of years   she nearly touched my hand
yes   I said   you were still alive

A Letter

My mother   because I don't write many poems
for you doesn't mean I haven't thought about you
every single day of these last fifty years   what
an avalanche of time   I can't begin to tell you
it's true though   in one or two busy decades   when
the children were young and noisy   when the war
and intense sexual love interfered   it's possible
I thought of you my mother less often   even then
suddenly in the evening I might see you for
a moment standing beside my father under
the Norway maple   your hair is at last cut short
and is becoming to your broad Slavic face
your hands are clasped lightly over the belly of
a summer dress   your arms nearly hide the fact
that you have only one breast   I watch my sister
snap that picture   my mother   I have not needed to
hold it in my hand

For Jan

The storm that entered his body
through the persistent dream of his prick
is still raging in him   he
tries turning his back to it   curling
into the kind of flower he
was once   a bud   a rolled-up be-
ginning   learning time under the
mother's heartbeat

The storm rages   suddenly rests
around the eye that stares
out the white barred
high hospital window into the white
city air   he watches the air   in this
minute's stillness he has decided
to go away from us   no   no not
into death   into a breathing
meditation on absence   years ago
he studied with the Chinese master in
the old neighborhood park   he moves his
little finger   ah   one of the
lovely defensive dances
of the East

Inside the eye   such stillness   a
door has opened and sunlight surprises
the household   the child runs out into the
city street   to play   to be a wild boy
to climb stoops and walls   to teeter
to race around the corner   the darkest
wind returns   oh   the mother cries   where
is he   where in the pouring rain   the
fury rolling off the city's roof   is he

hiding somewhere   as she taught him tucked
safely into the one two three four between
lightning and thunder

Later in the country hospital the storm
like war rages at groin and ear
lungs   even the bent knee   in the
country hospital   fear   withdrawal   ig-
norance   insult   that afternoon the war
which is the disease finds equilibrium
in steady agony   the man says   mother
when I ask   will you help me to die

In the morning the body itself becomes
impatient with torment's steadfastness
its refusal to make room for that
other idea   memory   pain absorbs
the street   mother   teacher   friend
sky   insatiable pain   leaving only
the work of breath   its stubborn
hopeless history

As in the storm of war   the body
of the man which was good is defeated
the disease which is evil is
defeated   the countryside rests
relieved   the hospital files some
new information   the nighttime
city streets are still our grids of
bravery and desire   in the
neighborhood park homelessness
has raised tents of black
plastic and clear plastic   the mother
and her son's friends visit the park
again and again   they bring sandwiches
coffee   scarves   hats

Luck

She looks at me   you're
lucky   you always were a
lucky person   what she means
is her life is hard   the man's
far off   the boy's mad

I make a joke   take it easy
there's time for me to be to-
tally wrecked   I grab her grief
jam it into the grief pack between
my shoulders   when my head
turns right or left   I know it

She laughs   mentions God   throws
her life up up into the sky
in fearful sleep   I see it   a
darkness widening among my
lucky stars

On the Deck

The old men are talking about sex
their wives turn away   sadness
pity follow   beyond the lawn
the women see the late September
garden   its wild cultivated flowers

Look how they fling themselves about
all those drastic last-minute colors
they laughed   they were shy   they walked
into the garden   though they were old
though they had said nothing yet
about love   they continued to talk
and tell until one man called out
in the voice of a book they'd read
it's late   it's dark   where are you

For My Daughter

I wanted to bring her a chalice
or maybe a cup of love
or cool water   I wanted to sit
beside her as she rested
after the long day   I wanted to adjure
commend   admonish   saying don't
do that   of course   wonderful   try
I wanted to help her grow old   I wanted
to say last words   the words famous
for final enlightenment   I wanted
to say them now   in case I am in
calm sleep when the last sleep strikes
or aged into disorder   I wanted to
bring her a cup of cool water

I wanted to explain   tiredness is
expected   it is even appropriate
at the end of the day

Therefore

When I am old
I will not be surprised as
Leon Trotsky said I would

I will not be surprised
for I have built my
Ship of Death as D. H. Lawrence
said I should

Therefore I can right now
as Barbara Deming cried
come dance with all your might
then I will live though I die old
in passion like a fool as
William Butler Yeats thought
would be right

Now I have learned in politics and
dream from William Blake
and that beloved Prince Kropotkin
whom I've read
with Robert Nichols in
the parlor and in bed
before we loved and sometimes afterwards
because the summer moon stands low
to glare on shadowed fields and in
this window makes such light   it is
the natural law as any child
would know of moon and love and night

In This Dream

In this dream the typewriter
is a piano   and I play
with unplanned accuracy and
such fluency you would think
I was a Southerner whose tradition
recommended continuous telling

or an Englishwoman home at last
writing   writing in English   you
would think that I was one
of the persons in charge of this
language   owning it from infancy
if this piano   on which I have learned
to play preludes nicely   if
this piano were a typewriter

Hand-Me-Downs

My love rests on the couch
in the sweater and bones of old age

I have stopped reading to look at him   I take
his hand   I am shawled in my own somewhat
wrinkled still serviceable skin

No one knows what to do with these
hand-me-downs   love them I suppose

weren't they worn in and out of
dignity by our mothers and
fathers   even our children in
the grip of merciless genes will
wear these garments

may their old lovers greet and
touch them then in the bare light
of that last beauty

Here

Here I am in the garden laughing
an old woman with heavy breasts
and a nicely mapped face

how did this happen
well that's who I wanted to be

at last   a woman
in the old style   sitting
stout thighs apart under
a big skirt   grandchild sliding
on   off my lap   a pleasant
summer perspiration

that's my old man across the yard
he's talking to the meter reader
he's telling him the world's sad story
how electricity is oil or uranium
and so forth   I tell my grandson
run over to your grandpa   ask him
to sit beside me for a minute   I
am suddenly exhausted by my desire
to kiss his sweet explaining lips

Walking in the Woods

That's when I saw the old maple
a couple of its thick arms cracked
one arm reclining half rotted
into earth   black with the delicious
hospitality of rot to the
littlest creatures

the tree not really dying   living
less widely   green head high
above the other leaf-crowded
trees   a terrible stretch to sun
just to stay alive   but if you've
liked life   you do it

Printed in the USA
CPSIA information can be obtained
at www.ICGtesting.com
LVHW091144150724
785511LV00005B/527